STANDARD
Storyline History
Book 1 by L E Snellgrove

Oliver & Boyd

Illustrations by Donald Harley, John Harrold, Nicholas Hewetson, John Marshall, Mark Peppe.

Oliver & Boyd
Robert Stevenson House
1–3 Baxter's Place
Leith Walk
Edinburgh EH1 3BB

A Division of Longman Group Ltd

ISBN 0 05 003666 1

First published 1986

© Oliver & Boyd 1986

Set in 14/20 Plantin 110
Produced by Longman Group (FE) Ltd
Printed in Hong Kong

Contents

Time Line   4

The Long, Long Voyage   6
(The sea journey from Egypt to Punt)

The Island of the Bull   18
(The legend of the Cretan Minotaur)

The King of Whole World   29
(King Darius of Persia)

The Brown and Green Island   42
(The legend of Ulysses and the Cyclops)

The Emperor and the Holy Man   53
(Asoka the Great, Emperor of India)

Buddhism   64

The Wall of the 'Only First'   66
(The Great Wall of China)

Which Hill?   76
(The legend of Romulus and Remus)

The Queen-Goddess   87
(Caesar and Cleopatra)

The Roman Empire   100

To Colchester!   102
(Queen Boudicca fights the Romans)

The Leather Boat Men   114
(Saint Brendan's sea voyage to North America)

BC (before Christ)

1500 1400 1300 1200 1100 1000 900 800 700 600 500

Queen Hatshepsut of Egypt

Battle of Marathon

Voyage to Punt

Greek story:
Theseus and the Minotaur

King Darius
of Persia

Roman story:
Romulus and Remus

Knossos destroyed

Greek story:
Ulysses and the Cyclops

Building of
Rome began

The band of colour beside each person shows how long he or she lived.

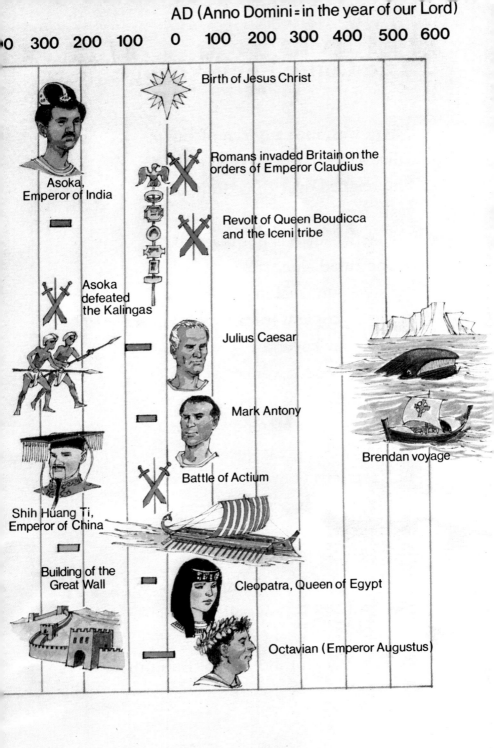

AD (Anno Domini = in the year of our Lord)

300 200 100 0 100 200 300 400 500 600

Birth of Jesus Christ

Romans invaded Britain on the orders of Emperor Claudius

Revolt of Queen Boudicca and the Iceni tribe

Asoka, Emperor of India

Asoka defeated the Kalingas

Julius Caesar

Mark Antony

Battle of Actium

Brendan voyage

Shih Huang Ti, Emperor of China

Building of the Great Wall

Cleopatra, Queen of Egypt

Octavian (Emperor Augustus)

The Long, Long Voyage

There was once a queen of Egypt
called Hatshepsut.
She reigned over three thousand
years ago.
   Hatshepsut was not married,
so she ruled alone.
This was unusual in those days,
as most people were ruled by kings.
Hatshepsut knew that some men
might not like a woman as a ruler,
so she dressed as a man.
Sometimes she pretended to be one!
Yet she was a great queen and
all Egyptians obeyed her.
   When Hatshepsut had been queen
for nine years, she decided to send
a fleet to the land of Punt,
near the mouth of the Red Sea.
This country is now called Somalia.
   "Build me five of the finest ships,"
she told her ship builders. "Build them

strong, for I hear that the seas are rough
and the winds powerful between Egypt
and the land of Punt."

The Egyptians loved boats because
they lived by the River Nile.
There were not many tall trees
in Egypt, so the Egyptians made
their boats from bundles of reeds
tied tightly together at each end.
But the ships Hatshepsut wanted
would have to be made of wood.
The ships were made from small
pieces of wood, fitted together
in the same pattern as we lay bricks today.

Such a ship might sag in the middle.
To stop this, the ship builders tied
a thick rope, thicker than
a man's waist,
from end to end of the ship.
This cable could be twisted tighter
if the ship began to sag.
Such ships were spoon-shaped and
very strong.

There would be more to this journey
than paddling down the River Nile.
The ships would need to
sail through a long canal
and then all the way down
the Red Sea to Punt. It would be
a long, long voyage.

When the ships were ready
and the sailors assembled,
each crew offered the gods
food and drink.
This was to please the gods and
bring the ships luck
on the long voyage.

The Egyptians believed that one god,
Osiris, had big, staring
eyes that could see everything.
So each of the five ships
had a big, staring eye
painted on its bow.
The sailors hoped that the god
would see in the dark and
show them the way!

The wide-eyed god Osiris.

The fleet sailed from Thebes.
At first each ship was rowed
out of the harbour.
The crowds cheered until the ships
were out of sight.
The sailors waved until the crowds
were out of sight.

Then they climbed the masts and
let the big sails flutter down.
Once in the open sea,
the sails could catch the wind.
    Waves rolled the ships
this way and that.
Each ship began to creak as
the sea pulled and tugged at
the tightly-fitted pieces of wood.
The thick rope running
from end to end of the deck
was screwed tighter.
The spoon-shaped ships,
each with a big, staring eye,
began to fly across the waves
like graceful birds.
The long, long voyage to Punt
had begun.

         ★   ★   ★

On board the biggest ship was Thothmes.
Thothmes was an important man.
Hatshepsut had told him to meet

the king of Punt and make friends.
Thothmes had the best cabin.
It was comfortable, and its walls
had pictures of gods and flowers
painted on them.

When the fleet reached the canal
the ships were rowed slowly through.
It was very hot and
the sailors sweated as they
pulled at the oars.
They were glad when they
came to the end of the canal and
felt the wind from the Red Sea.

Once again, each ship began
to rock and sway.
Five big, staring eyes rocked
up and down on five boats.
Five large sails billowed in the breeze.
Five ships began to fly across the waves
like graceful birds.

After many days the fleet
reached Punt. It was a land of
desert and hot sun.

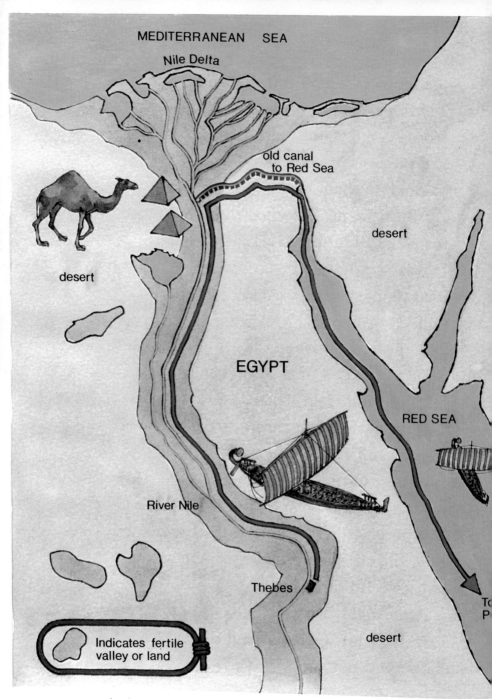

MEDITERRANEAN SEA

Nile Delta

old canal to Red Sea

desert

desert

EGYPT

desert

RED SEA

River Nile

Thebes

To Punt

Indicates fertile valley or land

12 Ancient Egypt, showing the route taken from Thebes to Punt. Find the land of Punt, now called Somalia, in your atlas and work out how far the ships had to travel to get there and back.

Queen Hatshepsut's boat on its way to Punt. The sailors are all rowing, so they must still be in the harbour, or perhaps the canal.

This royal ship seems to be bigger than Hatshepsut's trading ships. It was painted on the wall of an Egyptian tomb over 3000 years ago, so it is damaged in places.

13

The king of Punt, Pereka,
was pleased to see them.
Spies had told him
that the great queen of Egypt
was sending him gifts.

Thothmes went ashore to greet Pereka.
He gave the king rings, necklaces,
daggers and axes, as presents.
This pleased Pereka, for there was not
much metal in the land of Punt.

The king invited all the Egyptians
ashore, where they lived in tents
set up in the desert.
During this time the Egyptian
sailors and the men of Punt
became great friends.

Thothmes had a special present
for Pereka. It was a large,
stone statue of Queen Hatshepsut.

"Set it up by the shore,"
commanded Pereka.
"Set it up so that it faces
the great sea these brave

men have crossed to reach my land."

So the statue was set up
facing the sea.
Perhaps it still stands alone
in the desert,
scarred by sandy winds,
baked by the scorching sun.
Perhaps it still stands,
a shapeless lump of stone
after so many years.

Pereka gave the Egyptians gifts
to take back to their queen.
He gave them rare trees,
and ebony and ivory.
He gave them monkeys, dogs,
cattle and a live panther.
The ships must have been
very crowded on the voyage back!

Hatshepsut was very pleased
when her fleet was sighted
approaching Thebes.

Queen Hatshepsut's statue

The crowds cheered until the
ships were in the harbour.
The sailors waved until
they were safe in harbour.

Hatshepsut was even more pleased
when she saw the rare gifts
from the land of Punt.
She had the presents,
the trees and the animals
taken to her great temple
so that she could thank the gods.

The temple, which was cut into a
steep cliff, had hundreds of rooms,
courtyards and halls.
The queen must have been very proud
as she walked up the thousands
of steps which led to her temple.
When she was inside
she thanked the gods
for the safe return of Thothmes,
his sailors and his ships.
Later she had pictures of the ships,
and the gifts they had brought home,

carved on the walls of the temple.
When she died she was buried
in a room decorated with these carvings.

Some of the painted carvings from Hatshepsut's temple. What gifts can
you see from the land of Punt?

The queen never let her people
forget the long, long voyage.
Kings could go to war, win battles
and come home with prisoners
and the riches they had captured.
Hatshepsut was not allowed
to go to war because she was a woman.
So she sent her five spoon-shaped ships
on a long and dangerous voyage,
to make friends with a faraway king.

The Island of the Bull

In olden times the Greeks
told a story about a king
and a monster.
They said that far out
in the blue sea off Greece,
there was a lovely island called Crete.
It had steep mountains and
pleasant green valleys. It was
washed by a warm sea and
bathed in hot sunshine.
But it held a dreadful secret.

Many years before, said the Greeks,
the king of Athens had killed
the son of Minos, king of Crete.
Minos was very sad when he heard
the news. He was also
very angry and he sent his soldiers
to make war on Athens.
There was a battle and
the men of Athens were beaten.

To punish the people of Athens,
King Minos said that each year
the city must send seven young men
and seven young women
to Crete. Once on the island
they were taken to the king's palace.
The palace was spread out
over a gently sloping hillside.
Set like steps in the hillside
were buildings with rows and
rows of white and red columns.
Outside, the buildings glittered white
in the sun. Inside, away from
the sunny courtyards, there were

many dark places – rooms, cellars,
stairways, passages and tunnels where
the sun never shone.

The young Athenians were made
to go into these dark places.
They got lost and were eaten
by a monster with the body
of a man and the head of a bull.
The monster was called the Minotaur,
after King Minos.

Each year the king of Athens
pleaded with King Minos
not to kill the young people
in this horrible way.
Each year Minos said they must come
or he would make war on Athens again.

Then, one day, Theseus,
the son of the king of Athens,
said he would go as one of
the fourteen.

The king did not want his son to go.

"You'll be killed and eaten
by the monster," he groaned.

"No, father," replied Theseus.
"I'll kill the Minotaur
and save our people."

So when the next group sailed to Crete,
Theseus went with them.
As they stood proudly before King Minos,
the king's daughter, Ariadne, saw Theseus.
He was so handsome and brave
that she fell in love at once.

When the fourteen went into the tunnels,
Ariadne gave Theseus a sword
when her father wasn't looking.
She also gave him a ball of string
which he could unwind in the tunnels,
and so find his way out
if he did kill the Minotaur.

Theseus went in front
of the others, tiptoeing
along the passages and tunnels
and creeping through the rooms and cellars.

As he did so, he wound the string
out behind him.

At first there was no sound.
Then Theseus heard a roar
which echoed and re-echoed
through the passages.
It was the Minotaur!
But where was he?
Theseus hid behind a wall,
drew his sword and waited.
The bellowing grew louder and louder
until Theseus could hear
the thud of the monster's hooves
on the stone floor.
He waited until he could feel
the monster's hot breath as the Minotaur
galloped through the passages.

Suddenly, round a corner,
near the wall where Theseus was hiding,
came the fearful monster,
his eyes blazing.
He saw Theseus and tried to charge –
but it was too late.

Theseus' sword flashed in the darkness,
killing the Minotaur at one stroke.

For hundreds of years
Greeks told this story,
but many people did not
believe it. When travellers went
to Crete they found no king,
no palace, port or large town.
Had there really been a great palace
on Crete, they asked? Had there been
a palace with hundreds of rooms
and white and red columns
set like steps on the hillside?

Nearly a hundred years ago,
an Englishman named Arthur Evans
went to Crete to see if he could find out
why the Greeks had made up such a story.
Evans talked to Cretans
who told him that long ago
the island had been ruled
by a king who ruled the seas
and whose people worshipped
a bull-god.
One day, they said,
the town had been burnt,
the fleets sunk and the palace
knocked down by invaders
who came from Greece.
The Cretans took Evans to
a place called Knossos,
where a few stone walls
had been dug out of the ground.

So Evans told his workmen
to start digging at Knossos.
The year was 1900. Almost at once
there were exciting discoveries.

When the earth was dug away,
courtyards, rooms, stairways,
passages and tunnels
appeared like magic!
There *had* been a great palace
on the hillside at Knossos.

Evans found many wonderful things.
He found pots, vases, statues.
He found paintings on walls.
They showed young men and women
walking proudly in a line,
carrying dishes with
gifts of food for the gods.
They showed young women dancing.
And they showed young women
springing over charging bulls
by holding on to their horns.
There were also statues of bulls
and bulls' heads.

Because of what he had found,
Arthur Evans thought that the
Cretans *had* worshipped a bull-god
long ago.

He thought that was why the Greeks
had made up a story about
a monster, half bull, half man,
and a prince and princess
who fell in love.

But what of the invaders
who had come and conquered
this lovely island?
Some experts think that Knossos
was damaged and set on fire
by a great wave caused by an
earthquake. In 1400 BC there
was an earthquake on an island
called Santorin, about
ninety kilometres away,
which could have done this.

But what if the invaders
had been led by a king called Theseus?
Perhaps Minos the king, not
Minotaur the monster,
was killed by a Greek?
We shall probably never know.

The King of the Whole World

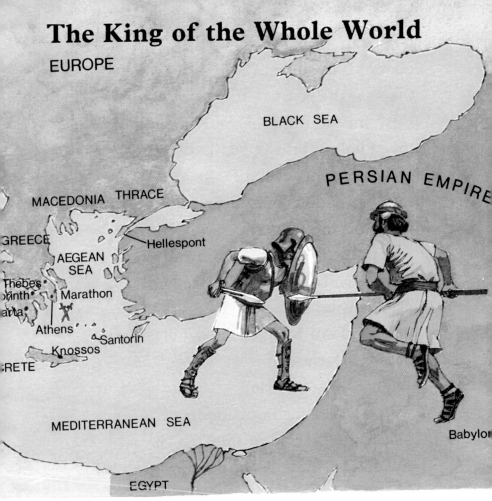

EUROPE

BLACK SEA

PERSIAN EMPIRE

MACEDONIA THRACE

GREECE

Hellespont

AEGEAN
SEA

Thebes
inth
arta

Marathon

Athens

Santorin

Knossos

RETE

MEDITERRANEAN SEA

Babylon

EGYPT

Ancient Greece and part of
the Persian Empire, which
stretched eastwards as far as
the River Indus.

Long ago, the land of Persia
(which we now call Iran)
was ruled by warrior kings
whose armies conquered many countries.

One king, called Cyrus, beat the
men of Babylon and
the men of Egypt.

"I am the Ruler of the Kingdom of
the Whole World,", boasted Cyrus.

A later king, called Darius,
sent his soldiers out of Asia and into Europe.
This was in 492 BC.
In Europe they beat the men of
Thrace and the men of Macedonia.

"I am the luckiest man alive,
because I am King of the Whole World,"
boasted Darius.

There was one land
which Darius hadn't conquered.
That was the land of the Greeks.

Today Greece is one country.
In those days the Greeks lived
in towns and cities,
each with its own king or
council of rulers.

One day Darius asked his generals
about the Greeks.

"Who are these men
who have no great king
to rule them?" he asked.

One general answered,
"There are many cities with many names.
There are Athens and Sparta,
Thebes and Corinth."

"Can these men of many cities fight?"
asked the king.

"Those who have fought them
say they are brave.
But they are also quarrelsome.
One town does this, another does that.
One says 'No' and another says 'Yes',"
replied the general.

"What of Sparta and Athens?"
asked the king.
"Will Sparta give in
and Athens fight?
Or will Athens give in
and Sparta fight?"

The general shook his head.
"Both will fight," he said,

"for the Spartans love war
above all things,
and the Athenians love freedom
above all things."
Darius was angry
when he heard these words.
"They shall obey me!" he cried.
"Send messengers to tell them
they must obey the King
of the Whole World!"

Darius' general had spoken the truth.
Some Greek cities said 'Yes'
and some Greek cities said 'No'.
But both Athens and Sparta said 'No'.
The council of Athens said
to the messenger,
"Tell your king that we are free men.
We would rather die than obey him."
Sparta had two kings, one to
defend the city, the other to go to war.
The two Spartan kings said,
"Tell your king he is wrong.

His soldiers cannot be the best
in the world for we,
the Spartans, are the bravest
and best soldiers in the world!"

Darius was very angry
when he got these messages.

"I shall send an army
to punish these proud Greeks!"
he shouted. "Send soldiers by sea.
Let them sail swiftly to Athens
and punish the city."

So, in the spring of 490 BC,
a Persian fleet sailed
across the sea to Greece.
Each ship carried horsemen
and archers, food, weapons
and tents.

When spies told the
Athenians the news,
the city council sent a
fast runner
called Pheidippides
to Sparta to ask for help.

33

Pheidippides ran very fast
but when he told the two kings the news
they shook their heads.

"It is festival time,
when we give thanks to the gods.
By our laws we cannot make war
at such a time.
But when the festival ends,
on the night of the next full moon,
we shall march at once to battle,"
they promised.

Back in Athens Pheidippides told the council,
"The Spartans cannot march
until the night of the
next full moon. We must
fight the Persians alone."

The Persians landed near Athens,
on a plain called Marathon.
They made camp and hoped
that the Greeks would come out
and fight them.
This was because it was easier

to beat an army
than attack a town
with strong, thick walls.

The Athenians came out
to meet them because they
did not want their city damaged.
Each Greek had armour
on his chest and legs.
He wore a large helmet
which almost covered his face
and he carried a sword,
a large shield and a spear
to throw at the enemy.
Such soldiers were called hoplites.

The Greek army
put their tents up on a hill
from which they could look down
on the Persians on the plain below.
By custom, a different general
led the army each day.
The general for the first day said,

"The gods are against us.
It would be foolish to fight today."

A Greek hoplite

The generals on the second,
third, fourth and fifth days
said the same.

On the sixth day
it was the turn of Miltiades.
Miltiades prayed to the gods
and then said, "We shall fight!
Today the gods are with us!"

The Greeks were excited
and shouted, "Today we fight!"
Each Greek put on his helmet.
He picked up his sword, shield
and spear and lined up.
The Persians, seeing this,
blew trumpets and got ready for battle.

The battle began with a nasty surprise
for the Persians.
They did not know that
the Greeks ran into battle.
Now they saw line after line
of plumed helmets, spears
and shields waving about,
as the hoplites ran at them.
The Persian archers fired their arrows,
which flashed into the air
and fell like rain.
But the Greeks were going so fast
that some arrows missed,
some stuck in the ground,
and some were caught
on the Greek shields.
At the same time
the Greeks threw their spears,
killing many Persians.
    The lines of hoplites
crashed into the Persian archers.
At close quarters the archers
had only daggers to fight

well-armed, well-trained men,
whose shields and helmets
made them difficult to kill.

The Persian general was worried.
He sent his horsemen,
thousands and thousands of them,
to the rescue.
Like the waves of the sea,
these lines of horsemen
crashed against the Greeks.
The Greeks in the middle,
still fighting fiercely,
moved back slowly, step by step.

A brave Persian saw this
and shouted,
"We win! We win!
They break! follow me!"

First one, then twenty,
then hundreds and hundreds
of Persian horsemen
spurred towards the middle
of the Greek line.
Too late they saw that the rows

of hoplites at each end
of the Greek line
were wheeling inwards.
The Persian army was surrounded.
It was a trap
set by the crafty Miltiades,
and few Persians escaped from
the flashing swords that day.

Miltiades took off his plumed helmet
and gave thanks to the gods.
Then he sent Pheidippides
to tell the council and people of Athens
the good news.

Pheidippides ran many miles
spreading the good news,
and died, worn out,
as he told the citizens of Athens.

Today, races called marathons
remind us of a famous battle,
a famous runner,
and a king who found out
that he was not the
Ruler of the Whole World!

The Olympic flame arriving in the Los Angeles stadium to start another Games. Find out about the Olympics in ancient Greece, and when the modern movement started.

The 1984 Olympic Marathon runners setting out, with 26 miles, 385 yards to go!

The Brown and Green Island

A Greek king named Ulysses
was sailing back from a war.
The war had been long and hard.
The voyage had taken many years.
Ulysses and his men had had
many adventures
and they were tired.

One day, the weary crew saw
a small island ringed with
green fields and crowned by
a tall, rocky mountain.
The island was like a
brown and green jewel
set in the blue sea.
It seemed a good spot to rest,
for there were sheep and goats,
orchards and cornfields on the island.

But Ulysses was not so sure.
A few days before, the goddess Athene
had spoken to him in a dream.
She had told him about an island

where fierce giants called Cyclopes lived.

"Beware the Cyclopes!"
the goddess had warned. "They are
cruel and ugly, with only one eye
in the middle of their foreheads.
If they catch you they will
gobble you up!"

Ulysses knew that in the blue sea
around Greece there were
many, many islands.
He hoped that this brown and green
jewel of an island was not
the island of the Cyclopes.

A statue of Athene. She has lost
her shield and spear, but still
wears her helmet.

That evening the Greeks
rested in a large cave
at the foot of the mountain.
At its entrance stood
a large stone, so big and heavy
that none of the Greeks could move it.

One by one the Greeks fell asleep.
The fire they had lit
smouldered and began to die.

Suddenly they woke up with a start.
They could hear a grunting
and a shuffling,
a panting and a puffing.
They heard a grunt
that turned to a growl
that turned to a roar.
 There, standing in the entrance,
was the biggest giant
they had ever seen.
He was as big as five ordinary men,
and in the middle of his ugly face
was set one fierce, round eye.
It was a Cyclops!

The giant was very angry
when he saw Ulysses
and his men.

"What are you doing
in my cave?" he roared.
"Are you pirates or robbers?"

Ulysses was bold and brave.
He stood up and faced the giant.

"We are not pirates or robbers.
We are soldiers on our
way back from a war.
The voyage has been long and hard.
We are weary and lost.
We hoped you would give us food
and treat us kindly,"
Ulysses told the giant.

At this the giant laughed and laughed
until the cave seemed to shake.

"I, Polyphemus, the Cyclops,
treat you kindly?
I shall gobble you up
for daring to come into my cave,"
he thundered.
Then, quick as a flash,
Polyphemus grabbed two Greeks
and gobbled them up.

Ulysses and his men drew
their swords and backed into
a dark corner of the cave.

Polyphemus gave the large stone a push,
sending it rolling across the entrance.

"Aha!" he cried. "We are
in this place together. If you
kill me you will never get out,
for only *I* am strong enough
to move the stone."

Polyphemus could not sleep
that night, for he was afraid
the Greeks would kill him
as he lay down.

The Greeks could not sleep
that night, for they were afraid
the giant would gobble them up.

In the morning Polyphemus
left the cave, pushing the stone
back across the entrance as he went out.

Ulysses was clever as well as brave.
He knew he would have to think
of a plan before the giant came back.

He thought and thought.
Then he said to his men,

"Pick up that big log
which the giant will use
to light a fire.
Sharpen one end to a point
with your swords."

The men were puzzled
but they did as Ulysses told them,
for in all the Greek world
there was no man as crafty
and cunning as their king.

"When the giant comes back,
he will come out of the bright sunlight
into the dark of the cave.
For a moment he will not see us.
At that moment we must push
this pole in his eye.
Then he will never be able to see us,"
Ulysses explained to his men.

So the Greeks picked up the heavy,
sharp log and held it on
their shoulders.
They pointed it at the cave entrance
and waited.

Soon they heard a grunting
and a shuffling, a panting
and a puffing.
There was a grinding noise,
as the giant pulled the stone
away from the opening.
Next moment Polyphemus stood
like a great tree,
with sunlight blazing behind him.
　　Quick as a flash
the Greeks drove the pole
into the giant's one eye.

There was a growl
that turned to a roar
and then to a scream.
"I am hurt! I cannot see!"
roared the giant.
"Who has dared to hurt me?"
"Noman!" shouted Ulysses,
as he and his men ran out of the cave.
"Noman has hurt you."

Step by step, bumping and stumbling,
Polyphemus found his way to the door.
Nearby lived his brothers,
Cyclopes as cruel and fierce as himself.
He called to them for help.
"Help me, brothers, help me!
Noman has hurt my eye!
I cannot see!" he howled.
"What did he say?"
asked one brother.
Another brother laughed.
"Take no notice of him,"
he said, "for he says no
man has hurt him."

The brothers laughed and laughed.

"Go to sleep, Polyphemus!" they shouted.
"You can come to no harm
if no man hurts you."

By this time the Greeks had reached
their ship and were rowing
away from the island.
They could see the angry giant
stumbling down to the beach.

Ulysses felt very pleased with himself,
so pleased that he took a risk.

"Ho there, Polyphemus!" he shouted.
"It was not Noman but the great
Ulysses who hurt your eye.
You may be big and strong
but you are stupid."

Athene, the goddess who had warned
Ulysses, was displeased by this.
It was she who had put the plan
into the proud Ulysses' head.
So she gave Polyphemus his sight back.
The great giant threw a huge stone,
which nearly sank the Greek ship.

Ulysses, proud, clever and brave
though he was, knew that he had
annoyed the goddess.
He was sorry for what he had done,
as his ship sailed away
from the island which lay
like a brown and green jewel
in the sea.

The Emperor and the Holy Man

There was once a mighty
emperor of India called Asoka.
He reigned more than two thousand
years ago.

He had lots of soldiers
and his men fought and won
many battles.
But Asoka was very cruel.
After a battle, the soldiers
he had beaten were killed.
Sometimes their women and children
were made slaves.

Everybody was afraid of Asoka.
High-born nobles were afraid of him.
Poor peasants were afraid of him.
His prisons were full,
and every day he had somebody
put to death.

When he went out hunting, thousands
of animals were killed.

Some were killed for food, but most
were killed for fun.

After a war, Asoka ruined the land
he had conquered.
Men and women were killed.
Their homes were torn down and
their crops were set on fire.
Sometimes only a few old women and
young children were left alive.

One day, as Asoka sat on his
fine throne, he boasted of his power.

"All the land, as far as horses
can gallop and as far as men can march,
is my land. Millions of people
are ruled by me," he said.

A noble, braver than the others,
rose to speak to the proud, cruel
emperor.

"There is one people and one land
you do not rule," he said.

Asoka was very angry when he
heard this.

"Prove that you speak the truth
or you will be put to death,"
he told the noble.

"The Kalingas, Your Majesty.
You do not rule the Kalingas," came
the reply.

This made Asoka angrier still.
because he knew it was true.
So far he had not managed to beat
the Kalingas.
They lived in a part of India
now called Orissa.

"Send an army!" shouted Asoka.
"Send the largest army in the world.
We will see if the Kalingas
dare to disobey me when they see
thousands and thousands
of my soldiers."

So a large army attacked the Kalingas
and this time they won.
Afterwards, thousands of Kalingas
were killed.
Their homes, cattle and crops were burnt.

When Asoka's soldiers marched away, they left crying women and children, sitting by the bodies of their menfolk and the ashes of their homes.

"No house now stands in the land
of the Kalingas," reported the general
to Asoka. "The cattle are dead,
the corn is just black stubble.
Smoke hangs over a dead land."

At first Asoka was pleased
at this news.
Then, one night, as he lay
in his comfortable bed,
he started to think about the Kalingas.
He thought of wives without husbands,
mothers without sons,
children without fathers.
He thought how hungry
they must be with nothing to eat,
and how cold with nowhere to shelter.
Next day Asoka forgot about
the Kalingas.
But that night, as he lay in bed,
he thought about them again
and he tossed and turned,
unable to sleep.
Each night the thoughts came back.
During the day his nobles
noticed that their emperor
seemed silent and troubled.
He didn't put so many people
to death.

He didn't go to watch his soldiers
training, or spend the day hunting.
Sometimes he asked the nobles
about the Kalingas.

"Does smoke still hang over the land?"
he would ask, or,
"How many children have no fathers?"
or, "How many people are starving?"

The nobles were puzzled.
They didn't know the answer
to these questions.
Asoka had never worried
about such things before.

Finally, Asoka sent for a holy man,
who spent his life telling people
about the Buddha and his teachings.
The holy man was afraid
that the emperor meant to kill him.
Asoka didn't like holy men
who taught people about Buddha
and they were not welcome in his land.

The holy man needn't have worried.
Asoka smiled at him

and told him to sit down.
This was a great honour, for people
had to stand before the emperor.
Then Asoka told the man
of his thoughts about the Kalingas
and of his sleepless nights.

"You have done bad things,"
said the holy man.
"The Buddha taught that men
must do nothing wrong or bad.
You must help people and
think only good thoughts."

Asoka looked at this man
who was so happy, although he was poor.
He looked around him at his splendid palace.
Its walls were hung with rich tapestries.
Its floors were covered with fine furniture.
He thought how rich he was
and yet how unhappy.

"You speak the truth, O holy man.
Go in peace," he said quietly.

Next day the emperor sent messengers
to the Kalinga people to tell them

how sorry he was for what he had done.

"Asoka the Great says it was wrong
to kill your cattle
and burn your houses and crops,"
said the messengers.

Later, Asoka had this message
carved on rocks so that people
passing by would see it.
He had it carved on stone pillars
which were set up by the roadside.
He wanted as many people
as possible to know he was sorry.
A few of these pillars
still stand today.
They tell us of the sadness
of an emperor who lived
more than two thousand
years ago.
Asoka decided that to say
he was sorry was not enough.
The holy man had told him
he must help people
and this is what he tried to do.

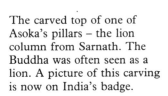

The carved top of one of
Asoka's pillars – the lion
column from Sarnath. The
Buddha was often seen as a
lion. A picture of this carving
is now on India's badge.

The emperor had good roads built
so that his people could travel
easily from one place to another.
Since India is a hot country,
he had trees planted along these roads
to give shade, and inns built
where travellers could get
food and shelter.
When the land was dry
Asoka had wells dug
to find water.
When people lost their homes
because of a storm or a flood,
he had new ones built.
When cattle died Asoka sent
fresh herds, and when corn
withered he sent more seed.

Asoka sent doctors to the sick.
And because of what he had done
to the Kalingas he gave up hunting
and killing animals.
He no longer ate meat.
Above all, he no longer made war.

His soldiers stayed at home
and there were no battles.
Peace and happiness replaced
death and misery.

Asoka never forgot that the holy man
who had given him such good advice
was a follower of the Buddha.
The old, bad Asoka had driven Buddhists
from his lands.
He had had them whipped,
put in prison or killed.
The new, good Asoka asked Buddhists
to preach all over India.
Some travelled even further,
and the people of China and Sri Lanka
first heard of the Buddha's teachings
from men sent by Asoka.

Before, Asoka had spread unhappiness
and suffering across his lands
like a fearful, raging storm.
Now he spread happiness and peace,
like a gentle wind which rustles the leaves
and sends ripples across a pool.

Buddhism

Asoka set his people a good example by following the Buddha's teachings.

The great Emperor sent Buddhist teachers to Sri Lanka, Burma and Thailand. Later, other Buddhist monks spread the teachings as far as China and Japan.

Today there are over five million people who follow the teachings of the Buddha. This is not a name but a title. It means 'one who knows' and was given to Gautama, an Indian prince, who gave up his riches to wander India teaching people to be loving and good.

A Statue of the Buddha from Sri Lanka. Sri Lanka was one of the first countries outside India to adopt his teachings.

Buddha speaking to his followers. Like Jesus, Gautama chose disciples to help him in his work. These men spread the truths the Buddha had discovered to other countries besides India.

Gautama was born into the Hindu faith. During his wanderings he tried to find out the meaning of life. He thought a lot and decided that people could find peace and happiness by obeying the 'Four Noble Truths' and following the 'Eight-fold Path'.

Try to find out more about the 'Four Truths' and the 'Eight-fold Path'.

In later centuries, millions of Indians returned to Hinduism, or else became Moslems. But Buddhism is still strong in Sri Lanka, Burma, Thailand, Japan and China.

The Wall of the 'Only First'

In China there is a long Wall.
It is very, very old.
People tell stories about the man
who had it built.
He was the Emperor Shih Huang Ti,
and he was so cruel
that everybody was afraid of him.

Before he built the Wall,
they say he flew to the moon
so that he could see
where it should be built!

Later, as thousands of peasants
worked at building the Wall,
Shih rode up and down
on a magic horse.
Every time the horse's hooves
struck the ground a new tower
sprang up.
The emperor carried a magic whip
so that he could beat the peasants
and make them work even harder.

Some say the Wall never ends.
It goes round the earth
and the ghost of Shih
rides on and on along it,
spurring on his magic horse
and waving his magic whip.

These are just stories.
But the Wall is real
and the Emperor Shih was real.
He reigned more than
two thousand years ago
and he was the first person
to rule the whole of China.
Because of this he called himself
'The Only First Lord of all China'.
He is still known as the 'Only First'.

Shih wanted a Wall
to keep out China's enemies.

"From the south we are safe,"
he told his nobles,
"for our enemies cannot cross
the high mountains of Tibet.
To the east we are protected

by the endless sea.
We are safe in the west,
for the people there
are our friends.
But to the north there are
savages who hate us."

Shih's nobles knew that the
emperor spoke the truth.

"These men from the north
must be kept out of our lands,
for they burn and kill.

A Mongol horseman

They are wild men who have eyes
but no faces," said the emperor.

These wild men lived by hunting
and raiding.
They killed people and stole their food.
It was difficult to catch them
because they rode fast
on small ponies.
Their flat noses made them
look as though they had no faces.
These were the Mongol tribes.
Shih wanted to keep them out of China.

Chinese princes in earlier times
had built short walls
to keep the northern tribes out.
Shih had these old walls
fitted into his great new Wall.

Year after year, peasants grew old
working on the Wall.
They dragged heavy stones,
cut rocks, made bricks and pounded clay.
They died of sunstroke in the summer
and freezing cold in the winter.
They died of overwork and illness.
Shih did not worry how hard they worked
or how many died.
He showed no pity.

Once, a wise man told Shih
that the Wall would never be finished
until ten thousand peasants
had been buried in it.
Shih found a peasant named Wan.
'Wan' in Chinese means 'ten thousand'.
The 'Only First' had the peasant Wan
buried alive in the Wall.

When it was finished, the Wall was
almost four thousand kilometres long.
It stretched like a great snake
along the jagged tops of mountains,
through lonely valleys and forests
and across quicksands and marshes.

"It is the most warlike barrier
in the world," boasted Shih.
"It will keep the men with eyes
but no faces out of China."

Thousands of soldiers guarded the Wall,
by day and by night.
When it was light they blew trumpets,
banged gongs and sent up smoke signals
if enemy soldiers were seen near the Wall.
At night they lit fires
all along the Wall,
stretching like thousands of lamps
across the dark countryside.
The fires were of many different colours,
red and blue, green and yellow.
It may be that these coloured fires
were the first fireworks ever made.

Part of the Great Wall of Chin

Long after Shih was dead
the 'men with eyes but no faces'
did break into China
and their leader became an
emperor, as Shih had been.
So the Wall did not save
the Chinese people, as the
'Only First' had hoped.

Today the Wall is empty,

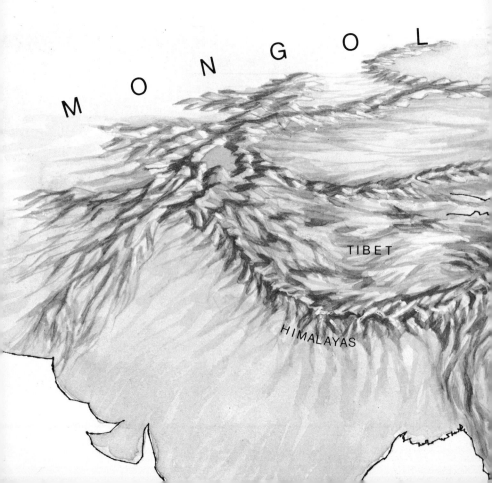

except for tourists.
No soldiers guard it.
No trumpets sound, no gongs clash.
At night, no fires light up
the countryside.
But people still tell stories about
the cruel man who had it built
and the thousands and thousands
of people who died building it.

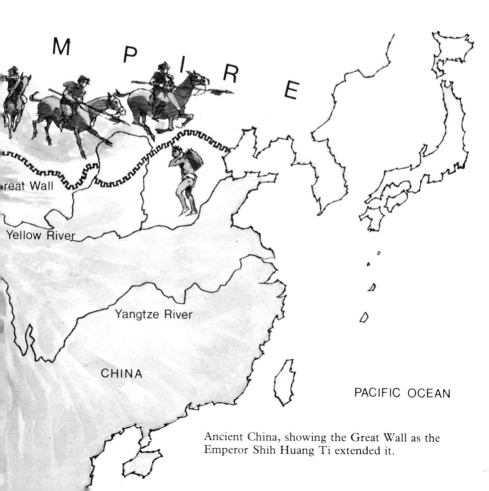

Ancient China, showing the Great Wall as the
Emperor Shih Huang Ti extended it.

Which Hill?

The Romans liked to tell this story
of how their city was founded.
Hundreds of years before, they said,
twin boys had been born
to a noble Italian lady named Silvia.
Silvia loved them very much
but she had a wicked uncle
who hated her.
The wicked uncle had Silvia
thrown into the River Tiber
where she drowned.
He put the two babies in a basket
and set them afloat on the river,
hoping that they would starve.
   It was pouring with rain
and the basket bobbed up and down,
nearly tipping the babies out
into the rushing stream.
Yet it was the rain which saved
the boys in the end,

because the river rose so high
that it flooded its banks.
The basket floated across the fields.
When the rain stopped
and the water went down,
it settled in a field near a fig tree.

At first the boys were all alone.
Then, said the Romans, first a woodpecker
and then a wolf brought them food.
The babies did not die.
They were found by a kind farmer
whose name was Faustulus.
Faustulus took them to his cottage
and he and his wife brought them up
as their own children.
They called them Romulus and Remus.

The wolf feeding Romulus and Remus.

Romulus and Remus grew up
to be strong and tall.
They became warriors
who saved people from robbers
and sometimes set slaves free.
Their deeds made them famous
and many other brave young men
joined them. Soon there were so many
that Romulus and Remus
decided to build a town
for their men to live in
when they were not away fighting.

In a way the brothers had been saved
by the River Tiber,
so they decided to build their town
on the hills near the river.

Romulus looked at what is now called
the Palatine Hill and said,

"That is the hill on which we shall
build our city."

Remus looked at another hill,
rising up near the Palatine Hill.
Today, it is known as the Aventine Hill.

"No, that hill over there
is the best spot to build our city.
There we shall be safe from
our enemies," he replied.

"No, that hill is best," shouted Romulus,
pointing to the Palatine Hill.

"You're wrong! That hill is best,"
replied Remus, pointing to the
Aventine Hill.

The brothers argued for a long time.
Then they went to Faustulus
and asked his advice.
He had once been a shepherd
on the Aventine Hill.
He loved both brothers.
He also knew how quick-tempered
and quarrelsome the two were.
He would not say which hill
he thought was the best.

Instead he said,
"Go to a fortune-teller.
He will show you what the gods
think about this matter."

So the twins went to
a fortune-teller. The fortune-teller
knew that the brothers were
quick-tempered
and quarrelsome.

"Watch the birds that wheel and swoop
over the river and the hills," he advised.
"See which way they fly.
Build your city where they fly."

Next morning Romulus and Remus
got up at dawn.
They looked at the river, the hills
and the sky, watching for a flock
of birds which would give them
a sign from the gods.
All day they kept watch,
as the birds wheeled and swooped
through the blue sky.
They watched until the sun set,
but no flock flew towards
either hill.

Next day the two brothers rose early.

Romulus climbed the Palatine Hill.
Remus strode up the Aventine Hill.
Each scanned the sky
for a sign from the gods.
The birds wheeled and swooped.
They flew up and down,
they dipped out of sight
behind this hill or that.

Suddenly Remus began to count,
"One, two, three . . . five,
SIX BIRDS!" he cried,
pointing towards the Aventine Hill.
Sure enough, a flock of six birds
hand flown over the Aventine Hill.

"The gods have given the sign,"
Remus shouted to his brother.
"See! They fly towards my hill!
It is there we must build
our new city."

Romulus was angry when he saw
the six birds and heard his
brother shouting.
He would not help Remus and his friends
as they began to dig
on top of the Aventine Hill.
Instead, he walked backwards
and forwards on the Palatine Hill,
looking up into the sky.
Perhaps more than six birds
would fly towards his hill?

Days passed. Remus' men worked
and Romulus watched.
Then, after a week, Romulus
gave a loud shout and pointed
into the sky.

"Look! Look! See!
Eight, nine ... twelve birds fly towards my hill!"

Remus stopped work and looked up.
The sky seemed empty to him.

"You're wrong!" he shouted back.
"There are no birds over your hill!"

Some men, who liked Romulus more
than Remus, said they had seen
twelve birds.

"We'll join Romulus," they said,
and left their digging on the
Aventine Hill. More men followed
and soon a city was being built
on the Palatine Hill.

Remus was very angry with his brother
and the men who had left him.
He, too, went over and began to argue
with Romulus.
The brothers' shouting could be heard
on the other side of the river!
Then Remus started to make
fun of the work that Romulus
and his men had done.
He jumped over the wall
they were building and cried,

"What a poor wall!
See how your enemies
will jump over it!"
This made Romulus furious
and he rushed at his brother.
It was a fierce and terrible fight.
In the end Romulus killed Remus
and let his body roll down
the slopes of the Palatine Hill.

Rome's coat of arms.
Try to find out what the letters SPQR stand for.

Now the other warriors had only one
leader. They helped Romulus build his
city and named it 'Rome' after him.
Roman fathers told their sons
this story, and the sons told
their sons.
When Rome became the centre
of a mighty empire
they told the tale,
and nobody harmed a wolf,
a woodpecker or a fig tree in the city.
Can you think why?

The Queen-Goddess

One day, long ago, a Roman general
came with his army to Alexandria,
the chief city of Egypt.
The general's name was Julius Caesar.
Caesar had just won a great battle
against other Roman generals
and now he was the ruler of
the whole Roman Empire.

Roman soldiers on a war galley, perhaps going home after a battle. Can
you see anything on the ship which shows that the men have been in
Egypt?

87

He came to Egypt to settle a quarrel.
The king of Egypt had died, and some
Egyptians wanted Ptolemy, the young son
of the dead king, to rule them.
Others wanted Ptolemy's sister,
Cleopatra, as queen of Egypt.
Who should it be, a king or a queen?

As Caesar wondered whom to choose,
a merchant came to see him.
He was carrying a large bundle
which he placed gently on the floor.

Caesar was puzzled. "What are you
selling? What is in the bundle?" he asked.

The merchant unwrapped the bundle
carefully. Caesar was used to being given
gifts. He expected gold, jewels,
precious stones, perhaps even a fine
vase or a statue.
Instead he saw a young woman wearing
a pretty dress. Her neck and arms
were almost hidden by pearl
necklaces and bracelets, and on her
head was a small crown.

"Who are you?" asked Caesar.

The woman rose to her feet
and faced the great Roman.

"I am Cleopatra," she answered
proudly, "the daughter of Ptolemy,
king of Egypt.
I was born to rule the land and sea
and to give laws to men.

The Pharaohs who came before me
now reign in heaven as gods.
I shall reign on earth and in heaven."

Caesar was amused by the trick that
Cleopatra had played on him.
He liked her beauty and her proud ways.

"You shall do all these things," he said.
"You look like a goddess, and you
shall rule like one."
Before long, Caesar and Cleopatra fell in love.
When Caesar sailed home to Italy
Cleopatra went with him.
They were very happy together.
They lived in Caesar's fine house
which stood by the River Tiber in Rome.
Word soon spread that Caesar
had brought home an Egyptian queen
and many men admired her beauty.
Some were not so pleased, because
they thought Caesar listened too much
to what Cleopatra told him to do.

"She has conquered our greatest general,"
they grumbled.

"Caesar has never lost a battle,
but he has lost his heart
to this foreigner!"
Cleopatra knew what was being said
about her but she didn't care.
What she did not know
was that some Romans thought
Caesar himself had too much power.
They didn't believe that one man
should rule the whole Roman Empire,
so they plotted to kill Caesar.
Caesar was warned of their plots
but he took no notice.
One day, in 44 BC,
they stabbed the great Julius to death.
Cleopatra was heart-broken.
She was afraid to stay in Rome
in case she, too, was murdered.
She fled to Egypt, just as a war
broke out between Caesar's friends
and the men who had killed him.
Caesar's friends won the war.
Two of them, Octavian and Mark Antony,

decided to split the Roman Empire
between them.
Octavian was to rule the west,
the lands of Europe, and live in Rome.
Antony was to rule the east,
the lands of Babylon and Egypt,
and live in Alexandria.
When Cleopatra heard this she decided
to give Antony a surprise.
It was to be very different
from the one she had given Caesar
all those years before.
Cleopatra sailed down the River Nile
to meet Mark Antony in a
gold-painted barge,
with purple sails and silver oars.

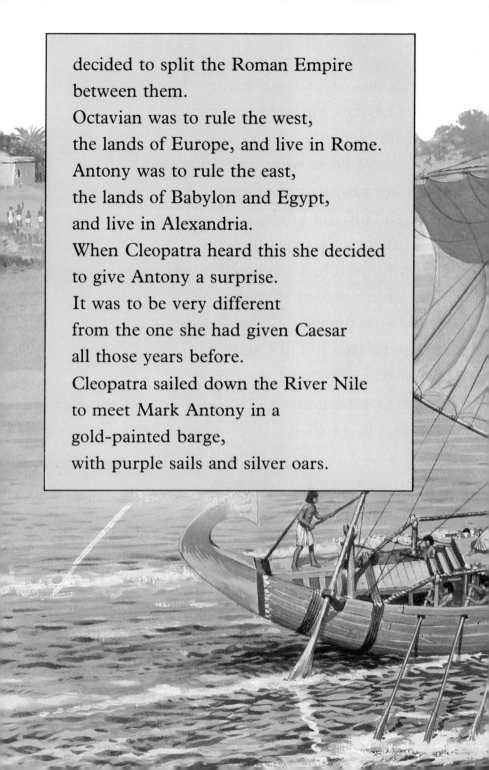

The river banks were crowded with people
who gaped at the wonderful sight.
Some even waded into the water
to get a closer look at their queen.

Cleopatra lay on a
couch of golden cloth.
Musicians sat at her feet,
playing flutes and pipes.
Servants stood behind her couch,
waving fans of peacock feathers
to keep her cool.

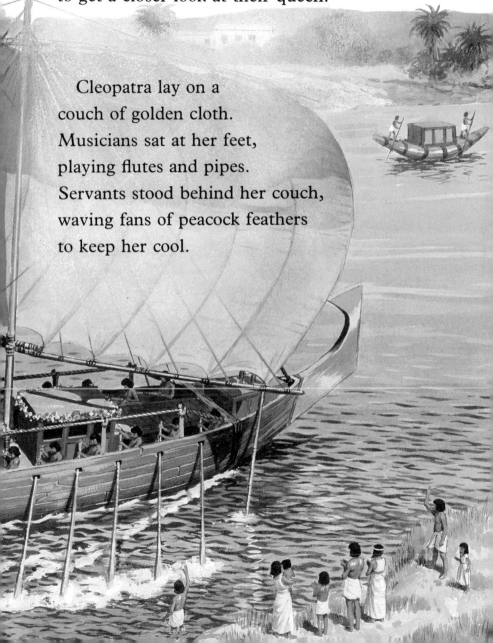

Caesar had fallen in love with a girl
who rose out of a bundle of cloth.
Mark Antony fell in love with a queen
who looked like a goddess
as she glided down the river
on a golden barge.

Cleopatra was clever as well as beautiful.
She knew that her new lover,
Mark Antony, would one day
have to fight Octavian.
"Only one man can rule the Roman world,"
she told Antony.
Antony did not want to fight.
He was as brave as a lion,
but before he had left Italy
a fortune-teller had warned him
that, though he would be great,
Octavian would be greater.
Cleopatra only laughed when Antony
told her what the fortune-teller had said.
"Don't worry, my love," she replied.
"Egypt is wealthy, Egypt is great.

With her soldiers and her money,
you can win a great battle.
Octavian will be beaten
and you and I will rule
the Roman Empire."
   But the queen who dreamed of ruling
earth and heaven was wrong.
Octavian's fleet beat Cleopatra
and Antony in a great sea battle
fought off the coast of Greece, near Actium.
Antony, who had ruled half the empire,
killed himself rather than die
a prisoner of Octavian.
   Cleopatra returned to Egypt.
She didn't want to go on living
now that Antony was dead.
So she gathered her treasure of
gold, silver, pearls, emeralds,
ivory and ebony, and shut herself
in a tomb with her servants.
   When Octavian reached Alexandria
he wanted to see the famous queen.
He came to the door of the tomb and said,

The Battle of Actium, where Cleopatra and Antony were beaten by Octavian.

"Don't kill yourself. Come to Rome
and ride beside me as my wife."

Cleopatra didn't believe him.
She knew that he was cunning and cruel
and would never forgive her
for loving Mark Antony.

"If I came to Rome," she replied,
"you would have me dragged through
the streets in chains before
I was killed."

Octavian went away.
He didn't care how she died.
That night a girl servant
came to the door of the tomb.
She was carrying a basket.

"What's in there?" asked a guard.
The girl lifted some leaves
which covered the top of the basket.
Underneath were large, ripe figs.

"Food for my queen," she replied.

The guard let her into the tomb.
Cleopatra smiled sadly when she
saw the girl.

She knew that there was something else
in the basket.

Hidden under the figs was a small,
deadly snake. Gently Cleopatra lifted
the snake and let it slide
up her bare arm. Suddenly it bit
her, burying its fangs in her soft skin.
As the poison flowed through her body,
Cleopatra lay back and
seemed to go to sleep.

Her servants knew she was not
asleep.
They began to wail and cry,
for they knew that she was dead.
Cleopatra, the last queen
of Egypt, had cheated Octavian.
She would never be led through the
streets of Rome in chains.
The Egyptians thought she had gone to rule
in heaven as she had ruled on earth.
And Octavian, whom Mark Antony had feared,
became the Emperor Augustus
and was worshipped as a god.

The Roman Empire

The first settlers beside the river Tiber were farmers and shepherds. They were often raided by nearby villagers, so they learned to be good fighters. They became so good at fighting that they captured all the towns and villages around Rome. Later, the Romans formed an army of well trained soldiers.

The Roman army conquered many tribes until Rome ruled the whole of Italy. This was the beginning of one of the largest Empires in history. Look at the map and make a list of all the countries the Romans conquered.

The Romans had central heating and hot baths long before us! The grandest Roman baths in Britain were at Aquae Sulis (Bath). The water came from a hot spring which people believed helped cure aches and pains.

The Roman Empire.

Because the Romans had such a good army, its generals were important men. The most famous Roman general was Julius Caesar. He won so many battles that he made himself ruler of the Empire. Other Roman leaders were afraid of his power, so in 44 BC they murdered him. This led to a war between those who had followed Caesar and those who had murdered him. Caesar's friends, led by Mark Anthony and Octavian, won the war.

Mark Anthony and Octavian divided the Empire between them. You can read about this and what happened in *The Queen Goddess*.

After his victory, Octavian called himself Augustus. He is thought of as the *first* Roman Emperor. The Romans were firm rulers who allowed the peoples they conquered to keep their own customs.

In AD 43 Britain was invaded by armies sent by the Emperor Claudius. (You can find out what happened to some of them in the next story.)

As well as fighting, the soldiers built roads, bridges, forts and towns as they marched north and west.

For nearly four hundred years southern England and parts of Wales enjoyed peace and prosperity under Roman rule. The Romans found the north of England and Scotland more difficult to conquer. In AD 122 the Emperor Hadrian visited Britain and ordered a wall to be built across northern England to keep raiders out. It is still called Hadrian's Wall.

By the fifth century the Empire had become too large for the Romans to control. Their armies left Britain and the Britons had to defend themselves against Saxon attacks from Holland and Germany.

101

To Colchester!

It was springtime in the year AD 60.
It was a time of great trouble
for the Iceni tribe, the ancient
Britons of East Anglia.
They had marched in their thousands,
warriors, women and children,
through the forests and swamps.
They had come with war-chariots,
spears and axes.
They had come with wagons and carts
laden with their goods, cattle
and food.
Now they stood silently,
waiting to hear what their war-leader
had to tell them.
Their war-leader was a queen.
She was a tall, fierce-looking woman
with long, fair hair reaching
almost to her knees.
She wore rough clothes dyed red,

yellow, blue and green.
Round her neck hung a large gold chain.
She held a spear in her right hand,
and when she spoke, her voice
was rough and harsh.

"Seventeen years ago the Romans
came to our lands," she shouted.
"We gave them what they asked for
and treated them well, because
we knew they were mighty warriors
whom all the world fears.
They haven't treated us well.
They must be driven away!"

The warriors cheered and waved their spears.

"We must do battle with them.
We'll take Colchester from them
and show them that they cannot
treat us as slaves," their leader went on.

There was another mighty cheer
from the warriors.

"We'll follow you, Boudicca.
We'll beat the Romans or die,"
they shouted back.

So Boudicca, queen of the Iceni,
led her thousands towards Colchester.

When the Roman Emperor Claudius
had conquered Britain, he had made
Colchester the chief town.
He ordered a big temple to be built
in the market place so that
Britons could go there
and worship him as a god.
  Many Britons were afraid of
the Romans, so they gave in and
worshipped Claudius.

Model of the temple of Claudius, Colchester.

One tribe that did this was the Iceni.
Their king, Prasutagus, didn't
want a war. His land
was rich and peaceful.
He didn't want Roman soldiers
to come, killing his people and
burning their crops.
His wife, Boudicca, didn't trust
the Romans, but she obeyed her husband.
She feared that the Romans would
take over the lands of the Iceni
once her husband died.

Prasutagus died in the year AD 59.
Just before he died, he wrote a will,
leaving half his gold
to the new Roman Emperor, Nero, and
half to his two young daughters.
Prasutagus had hoped that this would
please Nero and keep the Roman legions
out of his lands.

At that time, the Roman governor of Britain,
Paulinus, was away fighting the Welsh.
Paulinus was a hard but fair man.

He might have let the daughters
have half of the gold.
But Catus, the local Roman official,
was greedy and anxious to please Nero.
He sent all King Prasutagus' fortune
to Rome.

Boudicca was very angry
when she heard what had happened.
She told Catus that he was greedy
and not to be trusted.
For this she was beaten
with a whip by a Roman soldier.
Her two daughters were also
ill-treated.
The proud queen bore the pain
of the whipping bravely.
But she did not forgive the Romans
for ill-treating her young daughters.
Secretly, she swore that she would drive
the Romans, not only out of her lands,
but out of Britain altogether.

To do this she needed the help
of other tribes.

So she planned a revolt against
Roman rule at the very time
when Paulinus was away in Wales.

When the Britons took and burned
Colchester, Paulinus had just
captured the island of Anglesey
from the Welsh.

When a messenger rode into his camp
to tell him that nearly every
British tribe in the south
was fighting behind Boudicca,
he could hardly believe his ears.

"I have won the island of Anglesey
but I may have lost the island of
Britain!" he cried when he heard
the news.

And he knew where Boudicca's army
would go next – to London.
Paulinus decided to ride with his horsemen
to London to warn the people.
Riding fast, he might reach the city
before the Iceni and their warrior-queen.
His foot-soldiers, the legions which

never lost a battle, would march more
slowly. They could not reach London
in time to save it.

Boudicca had cried, "To Colchester!"
Paulinus cried out to his horsemen,
"To London – or we'll be too late!"

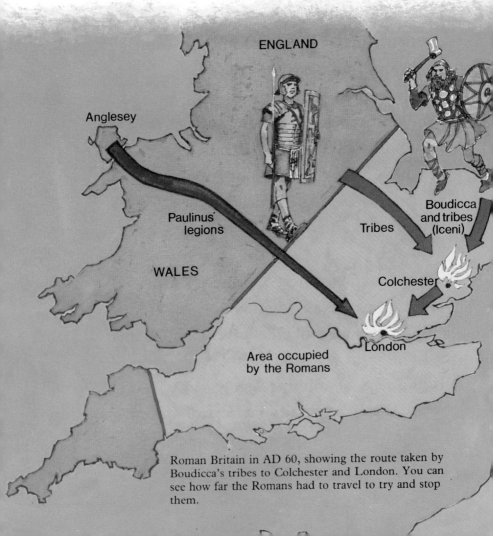

ENGLAND

Anglesey

Paulinus'
legions

Tribes

Boudicca
and tribes
(Iceni)

WALES

Colchester

London

Area occupied
by the Romans

Roman Britain in AD 60, showing the route taken by
Boudicca's tribes to Colchester and London. You can
see how far the Romans had to travel to try and stop
them.

Paulinus couldn't save London,
although his men arrived
before Boudicca's army.
He had to watch as the city
was burned and the people killed
by the wild warriors who followed
this queen.

As Paulinus watched London burn
he made a promise.

"Boudicca and all her army shall die
for this!"

Now it was a fight to the death.
Nobody knows for sure where
the final battle was fought.
Many think it took place at High Cross,
near the modern town of Nuneaton.
But wherever it was, Paulinus had his legions,
his terrible legions,
whose shields were like a wall,
and whose short swords cut and hacked
their way through the bravest men.

Boudicca made a mistake.
She fought with her wagons
lined up behind her armies.
This meant that if they lost the battle
there was no escape.

When the Romans came forward like one
solid wall, pushing and stabbing
from behind their shields,
the Britons were trapped.
They could not win
against these legions
who moved like
a slow triangle.

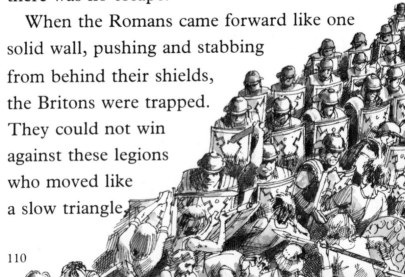

killing and trampling
everything in their path.
Men, women and children,
chariots and wagons, tumbled down
the hill as the Romans drove forward.

Boudicca knew now why the Romans
ruled a great empire.
She saw in action the terrible legions
who had beaten every army
they had ever fought.
She fled from the battlefield
whilst the Romans killed everybody,
just as she had done.
She fled as they burned everything –
just as she had done.

"I will not live as a Roman slave,"
she told the friends
who had fled with her. "I will not stay
to be tortured and put to death
by Paulinus."

So Boudicca, proud, brave Boudicca,
killed herself, and the Romans
ruled her lands after her death.

An artist's idea of how London must have looked when the Romans were in Britain.

The Leather Boat Men

Once there was a monk named Brendan
who lived at Clonfert in Ireland.
Not many visitors came to the monastery
but one day another monk, Barrind,
arrived for food and shelter.
Barrind and Brendan were old friends.
As they sat talking, Barrind
told a strange tale.
In those times men believed
there was a large island
far out in the western sea.
They called it the Promised Land
of the Saints,
because they were sure that holy men
lived and worshipped God there.

Barrind told Brendan he had
been to this land.

"It has rich crops, tall trees,
flowers and fruits. It has clear,
rushing streams and wide rivers," he said.

Brendan was interested by this story.
He had heard much talk of the
Promised Land but he had never met
anybody who had been there.

"I, too, will go to this land,"
he told Barrind.

"It will take a long time,"
replied Barrind.
"We sailed for seven years,
resting on islands during the winter."

"I shall do the same," said Brendan.

When Brendan told other monks
the story, they wanted to go too.
So they began to make a boat.
Irish boats in those days
were made from leather strips,
which were sewn together
and stretched over a wooden frame.
Brendan and his monks made
a leather boat with one mast and one sail.
They took oars so that they
could row when the wind was against them,
and food for the voyage.

The little leather boat
had a long and stormy way to go.

Brendan and his friends
sailed north and then west,
sweeping in a huge circle
across the western sea.
They used the islands they reached
like a person uses stepping stones
to cross a stream.
They rested first on a rocky island,
where the fields were dotted
with flocks of wild white sheep.
This was the Island of Sheep
and on it lived some monks
whose leader was called The Steward.
    The Steward was helpful.
    "You are going the right way,"
he told Brendan.
"Soon you will reach
Paradise Island where the birds speak.
When you get there, you will be
very near the Promised Land."

The following spring the monks sailed
away from the Island of Sheep.
One afternoon they saw a small bare island,
low and dark in the water.
They went ashore to rest for a while.
As they sat cooking some fish,
the island began to shiver and shake.
It was moving!

The monks ran as fast as they could
to their boat and rowed away.
The low, dark island moved away, too.
Then it began to sink.
At first Brendan could not
believe his eyes.
Some stories The Steward had told him
explained the mystery.
  "It wasn't an island at all!"
he cried.
"It was Jasconius, the great fish.
The Steward told me of such a beast."
  Sure enough, the 'island' rolled over,
flicked its huge tail,
and dived under the water.
Next day, when a fierce fish
with teeth like sharp knives
attacked the boat,
Jasconius rose up and bit the fierce fish
into three pieces.
Perhaps he had liked the men
who landed on his back?

Brendan saw wonderful things
on his voyages.
There were tall white pillars,
rising out of the sea like mountains
yet moving slowly through the water.
Today we call them icebergs.
There was a large island,
where the mountain tops let out
sparks, smoke and flame.
Even the sea around this island boiled.
The monks saw wild men running
along the beaches,
trying to sink their boat
by throwing lumps of hot metal at it.
One monk who had gone ashore
to look for food was carried away
by a column of red hot fire.
    "Row hard!" shouted Brendan.
"This island is part of hell
and these men are devils!"
    The monks rowed so fast
that they found they had gone
the wrong way.

Within a week they were back
at the Island of Sheep.
Brendan was very upset.

"We shall never reach the
Promised Land of the Saints," he moaned.

The Steward told him to cheer up.

"When you sail next spring
I'll come with you
and show you the way," he promised.

When spring came Brendan and his crew
set out on the last great voyage
to find the Promised Land.
This time they did not lose their way
because The Steward was with them.
They passed the white pillars,
the island where the birds could speak
and the island with the burning
mountains and wild men.
They even saw Jasconius,
who seemed to wave his tail as they went by!

After forty days they sailed into
thick, damp fog. Brendan was worried
in case they got lost again.

Brendan's voyage took him past icebergs
and erupting volcanoes on Iceland.

The Steward was pleased.

"This fog is a good sign," he told Brendan,
"for it circles the Promised Land
like a blanket to keep bad people away."

Dark day followed dark day
until the monks saw a bright light
through the gloom, like sunlight
at the end of a tunnel.
The light grew brighter and brighter
and, in a flash, the fog was gone.
There, before them, lay the Promised Land.
They saw its rich crops, tall trees,
flowers and fruit.
They saw its clear, rushing streams
and wide rivers.
It was just as Barrind
had told Brendan all those years before.

Brendan and his friends
lived happily in the Promised Land,
working and praying with the monks.
After some years a young man
came to Brendan as he lay resting.

He told him that all his voyages
had been part of God's plan
to show him the secrets of the ocean.
Now, said the young man,
it was time for Brendan to go home,
for soon he was to die.

Brendan did not mind.
He was an old man and he had
seen many wonderful things.
The voyage back was quick and easy
because a west wind blew steadily
behind them, filling the sail
and pushing the little leather boat
across the western seas to Ireland.
So Brendan came back to the monastery
at Clonfert after many years
of wandering, and died a happy man.

Brendan wrote a book about his
adventures. People who saw this book
did not believe all his tales.
How could a leather boat even float
or ride the rough seas so far,
they asked?

In 1975 a man named Tim Severin,
who had read Brendan's book,
decided to find out.
He built a leather boat
and found that it *did* float.
Then, a year later,
Severin and some friends
set off to follow the route
described by Brendan.

They, too, stopped in the winter
and sailed in the summer.
They landed on the Faroe Islands,
which, because the word 'faroe'
means 'sheep', they knew was the
Island of Sheep where Brendan
had met The Steward.
They visited Iceland, where volcanoes
belched out smoke and flame.
They sailed through some of the
foggiest seas in the world
off the coast of Newfoundland.
And, of course, they saw whales
and icebergs.

opposite picture
Tim Severin's boat
Brendan at sea. You
can find out more
about his adventures
and how the boat
was built in his
book, *The Brendan
Voyage.*

They even came to islands where
the birds sang so sweetly
that people might have thought
they were talking.

Perhaps the Promised Land
of the Saints was Newfoundland?
Perhaps Brendan was the first man
to cross the Atlantic from Europe
to America?
　Severin and his friends called
their leather boat *Brendan,*
after the monk of long ago
who had guided them on their long voyage.

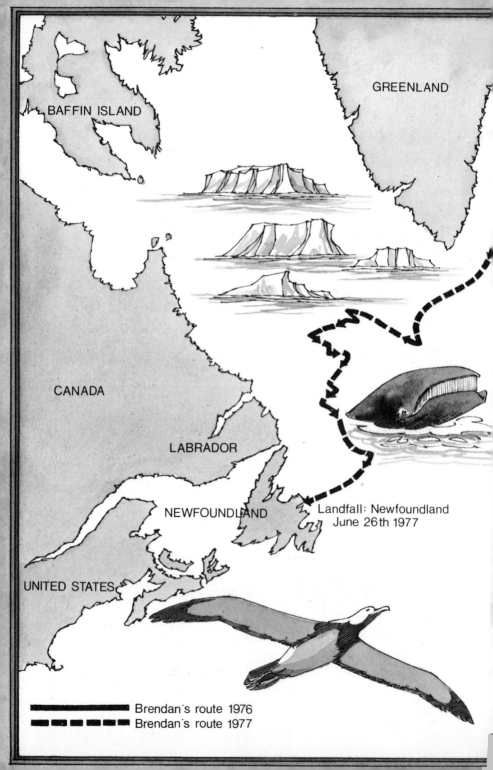

BAFFIN ISLAND

GREENLAND

CANADA

LABRADOR

NEWFOUNDLAND

Landfall: Newfoundland
June 26th 1977

UNITED STATES

Brendan's route 1976
Brendan's route 1977

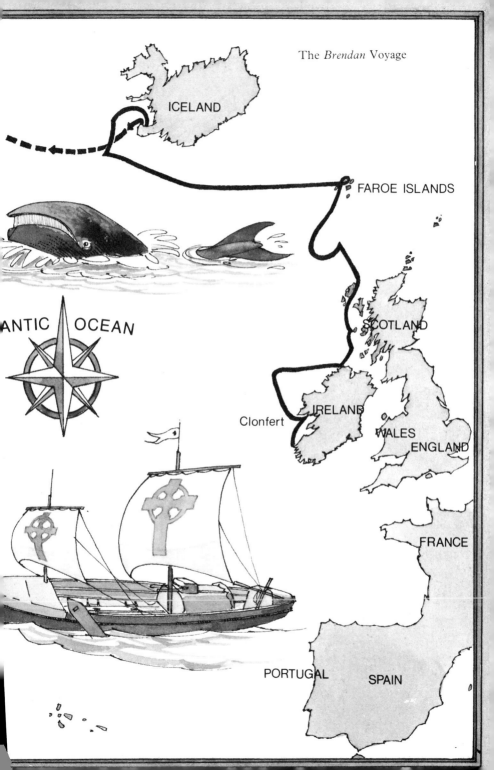

The *Brendan* Voyage

ICELAND

FAROE ISLANDS

ATLANTIC OCEAN

SCOTLAND

IRELAND

Clonfert

WALES

ENGLAND

FRANCE

PORTUGAL

SPAIN

Acknowledgments

We are grateful to the following for supplying photographs and giving permission for their use: All-Sport Photographic–David Cannon (above), Tony Duffy (below), p. 41; BBC Hulton Picture Library, p. 68; Bodleian Library, Oxford–MS Ashmole 1511, fol. 86v, p. 117; British Museum, by courtesy of the Trustees, pp. 18, 35, 43; Colchester and Essex Museum, p. 104; Sally and Richard Greenhill, pp. 69, 73; Hirmer Photoarchiv, p. 21; Mansell Collection, p. 87; Michael Holford, pp. 8, 12, 13, 49, 61, 64, 65, 77; Museum of London, pp. 109, 112-13; Susan Griggs Agency, cover and pp. 86, 101, 121 (two), 124; Unichrome (Bath) Ltd., 101; Werner Forman Archive, p. 17.